Welcome, Wombat

KAMA EINHORN
PHOTOGRAPHS BY **PHIL MELZER,
DONNA STEPAN & JACKY LING**

HOUGHTON MIFFLIN HARCOURT
Boston   New York

Library of Congress Cataloging-in-Publication Data
Names: Einhorn, Kama, 1969-author. | Melzer, Phil, illustrator, photographer. | Stepan, Donna,
illustrator, photographer. | Ling, Jacky, illustrator, photographer
Title: Welcome, wombat / Kama Einhorn ; photographs by Phil Melzer, Donna Stepan, and Jacky Ling.
Description: Boston ; New York : Houghton Mifflin Harcourt, [2018] |
Series: Sanctuary stories | Audience: Ages 7-10. | Includes bibliographical references.
Identifiers: LCCN 2017043188 | ISBN 9781328767028
Subjects: LCSH: Wombats--Conservation--Juvenile literature. | Melzer, Phil--Juvenile literature. |
Stepan, Donna--Juvenile literature. | Sleepy Burrows Wombat Sanctuary--Juvenile literature. | Wildlife
rehabilitation--Australia--Juvenile literature. | Wildlife rescue--Australia--Juvenile literature.
Classification: LCC QL737.M39 E36 2018 | DDC 599.2/4--dc23
LC record available at https://lccn.loc.gov/2017043188

Manufactured in China
SCP 10 9 8 7 6 5 4 3 2 1
4500725208

This book is based on the true stories of rescued wombats, and it's full of real facts about these wild animals. But it's also "creative" nonfiction—because wombats don't talk, at least not in ways that humans can understand! Some wombats in this story are combinations of several different ones, and certain details, including locations, events, and timing have been changed, and some human dialogue has been reconstructed from memory.

This book is not a manual on how to rescue wildlife, or provide any actual directions on caring for wombats or any other species. Every situation and every animal is different. If you see an animal in trouble, contact a licensed wildlife rehabilitator right away.

For Donna Stepan and Phil Melzer,
who have opened their home and hearts
to so many wombats . . . and to me.

CONTENTS

HOPE & HAVEN:
ANIMAL SANCTUARIES

A sanctuary is a safe place where living beings are kept away from harm and are free to be themselves.

Humans have created animal sanctuaries—protected places for injured, orphaned, or threatened animals. In sanctuaries, animals prepare to return to the wild. If that's not an option, the animals spend the rest of their lives there, in as natural a habitat as possible.

Most animal sanctuaries exist because of harm done by people. Humans may have built houses or buildings that force animals out of their homes. They may have put roads through animals' territories, so wildlife is more likely to be hit by cars. Some people consider particular animals to be pests. For instance, some farmers trap and kill wombats because they eat their grass and dig holes that destroy the fences that keep their farm animals on their property. Extreme weather events like droughts, heat waves, and floods are also threats.

The people who run sanctuaries are serious about

their work, but they all wish that they didn't have to do it in the first place. They wish there was no more need for these places, that the world was safer for animals.

There's plenty of heartbreak in any sanctuary's story, but there's also lots of happy news. Most sanctuary owners teach people about local wildlife, and they explain ways to protect animals and share the land with them. The more you know about why sanctuaries are important and what people can do to help, the better off all animals—both in your neighborhood and way across the planet—will be.

SANCTUARY STEPS

Each sanctuary is different, but they all do some or all of the following things, in the order below. Sleepy Burrows Wombat Sanctuary handles all four phases:

- **Rescue:** Humans step in, remove animals from harm, and bring them to safety. Rescue situations are usually emergencies.

- **Recovery:** Licensed wildlife caregivers treat the animals for injuries or illnesses, create a recovery plan, and let them rest and heal.

- **Rehabilitation:** The caregivers encourage the animals' natural instincts. Some things have to be taught, some the animals just know. Sometimes animals learn from one another.

- **Release:** Using a careful (sometimes very slow!) process, caregivers help animals return to their natural habitats whenever possible.

PART 1
RESCUE
Helping Hands

PiNKY WiTH A PROBLEM

Oh, hi, tiny thing. Welcome to Sleepy Burrows Wombat Sanctuary. I'm Chance. I'm a wombat, too. I'm two years old, and I've been living here for more than a year.

This is me, Chance.

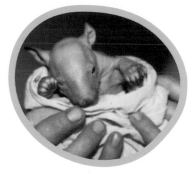

Look at you, mate! You're just a teeny joey—that's a baby wombat!

Don't worry. I'll explain everything about being a wombat, and I think you'll be pleased to learn how totally awesome we are. But first, here's what's going on.

The two humans who brought you here are Donna and Phil. I knew you were coming because soon after sunset, the phone rang and Donna called out that there was a joey who needed help. It was almost my feeding time when she and Phil rushed out, but I didn't mind waiting, as long as I got my carrots soon. No worries. I've been snacking all day anyway.

Donna and Phil
know all about
helping wombats
in trouble.

I know you must be scared, little mate. I was
scared when I arrived, too. I'll tell you more
about that later. Right now it's all about you.

From all the human yapping, I've pieced your
story together. You probably don't remember
much. See, your mum was crossing the road
to go find more grass to munch, and she got
hit by a car that was going too fast. Then
your mum . . . well, your mum died right away.

I'm sorry, buddy. Maybe you didn't realize.

The truth is, lots of us wombats and other wildlife get hit by cars. We don't see very well. Our sense of smell is excellent—we can smell the difference between twenty different kinds of grass. But we can't smell cars coming, now can we?

The couple in the car was so upset. They got out, looked at your mum's belly, and saw her pouch. They could tell you were wiggling around in there. It's a good thing they checked, because even after our mums die, we can stay alive in their pouch for five days.

We start our lives in our mum's pouch, like koalas and kangaroos. This makes us a special kind of mammal called a marsupial.

The couple searched for "wildlife rescue" on their phone and found Sleepy Burrows. Donna jotted down your exact location on the back of an unopened envelope on her desk. It was an hour's drive, and when they arrived, Donna pulled you carefully out of your mum's pouch with a piece of clean cloth. She knew the cloth would get your mum's smell on it and keep you calm when you were swaddled in it. Then they wrapped you again in one of Phil's flannel shirts. Phil carried your mum's body to the back of their truck, so he could bury her later. He gently set her down and covered her in an old blanket.

The couple thanked Phil and Donna and hugged them. "Is she going to be okay?" the woman asked, her voice trembling. "I hope I didn't cause *two* deaths!"

All of us wombats live in Australia.

"We'll take good care of this little one,"
Donna said. "Thank you for checking the
pouch, and for calling us. There are never
any guarantees, but call us in a year's time,
and hopefully you can visit us, to see how
she's grown." Phil put you, all bundled up,
inside his own shirt, close to his skin, to keep
you warm as Donna drove home.

We sleep all day in burrows (underground tunnels).
The sanctuary's motto: "Where wombats dominate . . .
and humans accommodate!"

And here you are. If all goes well, you could
live for five years in the wild. It could be a
good life out there. Donna tries to make it
happen for all of us. Some of us don't return
to the wild, but lots of us do. Those of us who
stay might live until age fifteen, which tells
you just how dangerous the wild can be.

"Wombat" comes from an Aboriginal word,
"wambad." Sometimes Donna and Phil give

us native Aboriginal names, like Dakara ("hard ground") or Yhi ("goddess of light"). Aboriginals are the native people who were here long before European settlers came here hundreds of years ago.

Our habitat is grassy, hilly, and full of eucalyptus forests. The land can be dusty or muddy, depending on the season. There are cool trees around us called ghost-gums, with smooth white—or even pinkish!—bark. They're called ghost-gums because you can see them in the dark. The bark feels a little powdery, and the long light green leaves smell sweet and minty. I hope you'll smell them someday.

All you have to know now is that you're in good hands. Donna's been doing this since 2004. Running the sanctuary is her full-time job (it's Phil's job, too, but he has another job fixing heaters and air conditioners). Donna and Phil are wildlife rehabilitators, with special training and a license from the government. They've learned from other caregivers, and they've *really* learned by watching us closely and trying different things. They often wind up teaching our vet, Dr. Joseph, about us!

Donna and Phil take care of about thirty of us at a time. Some are little pinkies like you; some are bigger; some are fully grown. Some live inside; some live outside. When our mums aren't here to show us how to live in the wild, Donna and Phil help us learn to be "normal" wombats so we can live in the bush, where we belong.

We share our habitat with kangaroos, wallabies, koalas, wallaroos, echidnas, platypuses, quolls, emus, and even more native Australian creatures. Strange thing, most Australians never get to see even one of us wombats in the wild. We're good hiders.

THE SONGLINES

Aborigines believe in songlines, or dreaming tracks—invisible paths that stretch and crisscross all over Australia.

They believe that before there were people, giant beings wandered Australia, singing the name of everything that crossed their paths. These story-songs are like maps with every detail of the landscape and animals. If people know the songs, they can navigate thousands of miles without getting lost.

Aborigines believe that children inherit traits from the songline running through their birthplace. For example, if you are born on a wombat songline, you may have some characteristics of the wombat, like a habit of pushing your way through obstacles and never giving up.

Donna thinks that wombat songlines run through Sleepy Burrows and that wombats follow the wombat dreaming tracks of their ancestors till they get here, knowing they'll be safe.

Donna and Phil help kangaroo joeys and birds, too. And when they see shingle-back lizards on the roads, they pull over, pick them up, and bring them back to the sanctuary so they won't get hit by cars. But mostly, they help us.

Our closest relatives are koalas, which is weird because koalas are all about being *up, up, up* in trees and we're all about being *down, down, down* in the earth.

We're called "bare-nosed wombats" or "common wombats," but there are two

When a koala walks on all fours, it's easy to see how we're alike.

other species: the northern hairy-nosed, which are almost extinct, and the southern hairy-nosed, which are also having a pretty rough go of it. Both have very hairy noses, obviously. To tell you the truth, us bare-nosed wombats aren't doing much better—there aren't as many of us as before, because of more roads and human buildings in our habitats.

Some wombats at Sleepy Burrows were once kept as pets. As you grow, you will understand what a truly terrible idea this is. Humans want us to walk on leashes and visit the supermarket and hang out with their friends, and they expect us to stay up during the day and sleep at night, just like them. That's torture for us, because we're nocturnal—we sleep all day and are up at night.

Since we'd stay with our mums for almost

two years in the wild, and because we need bottles every two hours when we're pinkies, we enjoy our "human families" . . . at first. But once we get big, watch out! We can become destructive and aggressive; it's just our natural instinct kicking in. That's when the humans who wanted cute little pet joeys decide we're "becoming a problem" and they dump us in the bush, where we wouldn't know

Pecan and Pistachio were indoor pets, so their paw pads were silky-soft when they got here. But paw pads should be tough—wait till you see how tough mine are already!

anything about how to survive. If we're lucky, they bring us to Donna.

There are other creatures at Sleepy Burrows, too—like Stella and Bella. Stella is our guardian angel. She's a Maremma—a sheepdog bred for protecting flocks of sheep from wolves. But guess who else Maremmas can protect? Yup. Us.

I think Stella looks like a brave lion.

Many of the wombats Donna has helped have been released and now live in the wild on the sanctuary property. If they're sick or hurt out there, Stella finds them (the sanctuary property is so big that two humans just can't keep an eye on the whole place). Stella's another pair of eyes and ears for Donna, especially when she and Phil are trying to get some sleep. When Stella finds a wombat who needs help, she barks in a special way and lies down near the wombat or its burrow until Donna or Phil arrive.

Stella plays with the young wombats. She knows everyone's smell. She's family, and I definitely wouldn't say that about any other dog that came to visit—I'd growl or shriek.

Every morning, Stella makes sure that Dawn, a very old wombat who lives in the shed, is doing okay. Stella gives a special bark that tells Donna "All is well." Then she walks the property, like a guard.

Bella is a German shepherd who mostly looks after the humans. "Bella" and "Stella" rhyme, so that when the humans call one dog, both come. Donna and Phil need the two of them!

"Bella" means "pretty"!

For joeys, this place is like wombat school. Donna and Phil are great teachers. But some things you have to learn from another wombat. So I, Chance, have taken on the job.

CHAPTER 2

CHANCE
THE CHATTER-BAT

First things first. Donna is preparing you a warm bottle. Don't worry, the milk will taste a lot like your mum's. Donna knows what she's doing. She's rescued almost *one thousand* of us so far.

You can relax and let Donna fill your belly while Phil's in the laundry room selecting your cloth pouch. The pouches are organized by size, stacked on the shelf just waiting for the next little newcomer. Donna and Phil have used them for hundreds of babies. You're so tiny and cold that you need two of them to stay warm.

Maybe it'll relax you to curl up and listen to me. To Donna and Phil, I just sound like this:

Barron having one of his first sanctuary meals.

Grunt grunt. Sniff sniff. Snuffle snuffle. Snarl snarl. Squeal squeal. Chomp chomp. Grumble grumble. Yip yip yip! They can't even be sure what all these sounds mean.

The humans call me a "chatter-bat." I call myself wise. I do know a thing or two about

being a wombat, and I'll tell you everything.
You'll need all the help you can get, and, like
Stella, I'm the eyes and ears of this place.
(Actually, I'm the *nose* and ears, because
we're better at smelling than seeing. But I
listen to everything the humans say—our
ears may be tiny, but they work fine.)

When you were born, you looked like a shiny
pink jelly bean (that's why you're called
a pinky)! You climbed up your mum's belly,
smelling your way to the opening of her
pouch, and you crawled right in. It became
your dark, warm, safe home. You attached
your mouth to her nipple so you could drink
her milk, and you grew. Now you weigh as
much as three sticks of butter!

I'm sure you remember that mums' pouches are
snuggle chambers, and being inside is like being
hugged tight every single second of every

single day! Pouches are pink and hairless inside. As we grow, the pouches grow, too.

Pouch openings face backward, toward mums' back legs. Grown-up wombats spend so much time digging that if babies faced forward, there would be some very dusty,

Veg, with baby VB in her pouch.

Baby June resting in her mum Veg's pouch.

muddy joeys. As we grow, we start to move around in the pouch and peek our heads out. When mum grazes on grass, we can stick our heads out and do the same. We can also flip over, poke out our back legs, and go pee and poop! Our mums have a round muscle that keeps us in while they run or jump.

If all goes well (and it certainly did not go well at first for you or me), we leave the pouch after about six months. But guess what? A wombat can always change its mind and *crawl right back in*, and might do this for a few more months (because why not? It's warm and cozy in there!). When we're out and about and we lose sight of our mums, we make a little sound like *huh-huh*; our mums make the same sound right back to tell us that we're safe.

Some joeys just don't want to leave the pouch, and their mums' bellies may drag along the ground. A mum can keep her joey from getting back in, but she can't force her joey out! This seems to me like a very clever trick of nature. Even after we leave the pouch for good, we stay with our mums for almost another year.

I bet you miss your mum's pouch, little buddy.

Oh man, I *loved* my mum's pouch. I was perfectly happy inside it, but I was also getting big enough to come out of it and explore our burrow, and when we were outside, I could poke my head out to nibble some grass and sniff the night air. I wasn't a pinky anymore; I already had my fur. Then, one starry night when I was about seven months old, an awful thing happened, and I never got to be inside my mum's pouch again.

Here's what happened: Some hunters and their dogs came toward my mum as she grazed. I had never heard a human's voice or a dog's bark. The dogs were supposed to be helping the hunters find pigs, but instead, they hurt my mum badly, and she stopped moving. Then she died. Because I was in her

pouch, I'd gotten bitten, too. I wiggled out
and tried to scoot away from those dogs, but
I couldn't. I was too small and slow.

Then I saw the hunters' big leather boots in
the moonlight. One hunter scooped me up
off the ground. He lifted me so, so high. He
had strange-smelling, enormous hands.

The hunters seemed to feel bad. They
brought me to someone's house, but the
people there didn't know what to do. They
put me in their cold, empty bathtub with
towels and wet dog food, which I couldn't
eat. The house was loud, so I couldn't sleep
when it was light, like I was supposed to.

Finally someone asked Donna and Phil to
help. The next thing I knew, I was being
wrapped and bundled in a blanket and lifted
up again by more strange hands. A human

voice said, "Okay then, beautiful boy. Let's get you healthy." That was Donna, of course. She had a gentle voice, but now I was afraid of any human. She put me in the truck between her and Phil and tucked some more towels around me.

Once we got to Sleepy Burrows, they examined me. My dog bites were bad and my tummy was messed up. Donna handled me softly, but she was angry that I hadn't been taken care of earlier. Their scale showed that I weighed much less than I should. Phil held me as Donna cleaned my wounds, then she put me in a warm cotton pouch and put that pouch inside another pouch. She brought me into the dark laundry room to help me calm down and rest. She put me in a small box on the floor with a hot-water bottle.

The night I arrived, I was a mess.

Donna sat close to me all night long. Her human smell filled my huge nostrils and the sound of her voice floated in the air. Both were strange at first, though by the end of the next day I loved them. Donna had a pillow and a blanket and she slept on and off. When she was awake, she stared at me and spoke sweetly. She told me I had come to the right place, and promised I'd be safe.

She fed me warm bottles, but if I drank too much my belly would hurt. So I got just a few sips, once every hour. She timed it with a little alarm on her phone that sounded like crickets. The room slowly got brighter as the sun rose, and then Phil poked his head in. "How's the little fella doing?" he whispered.

"Too soon to tell, I'm afraid." Donna yawned. "He's not able to digest too much. The dog bites are worse than they seemed, I think." She sighed softly.

"Well, we'll give him a chance, won't we," Phil said. "Hey, maybe that should be his name. Chance, who got a second chance."

Donna smiled. She gulped down her coffee, grabbed a crumpet, and carried me back into the truck. She drove me right to Dr.

Joseph, who gently examined me, gave me
a shot, then stitched me up where the dogs
had bitten me (luckily, I've forgotten most
of that part!).

"He's in a pretty bad way, Donna," he said
as she tucked me back into my pouch.
He seemed very serious. "There'll be no
surprises if this one doesn't make it."

"I know," Donna said quietly. "But we give all
of them a chance, don't we?"

The vet's smile was warm and sad, and his
eyes were kind. "The best chance he has is
with you, my friend," he told her. "Just work
all the magic you've got." He gave Donna a
packet of antibiotics to keep my wounds
from getting infected, and he moved his
face close to mine. "Good luck, little guy,"
he whispered.

Back "home," I was so weak I couldn't even stand. I could only lie on my tummy.

Slowly, my belly started getting better and my wounds healed. I began to perk up a bit and become interested in what was happening around me. Donna started taking

Mostly, I hid in my cloth pouch and thought of my mum.

me outside in my pouch for fresh air, a
few minutes at a time. The air smelled just
like my world before everything changed.
Donna put her tiny kisses on my big,
leathery nose.

I started eating solid food. First, I tried some
grass that Donna brought in. Then I started
eating wheat biscuits (called bikkies),
carrots, sweet potatoes, and oats. I also
liked the crunchy "wombat granola," which
is really horse feed; it's made from seeds,
beans, barley, corn, grass, oil, and molasses,
and it has pellets full of vitamins and
minerals. I've seen wombats open cabinets
and chew through doors to get to a giant bag
of wombat granola!

I still remember my first taste of bikkies.
Donna put one on the kitchen floor so I could
smell it. I used my nose to shove it around a

bit, and I touched it with my lips, but I didn't swallow it. It was very dry. But Donna kept putting my bikkie on the floor every day, and now they're my favorite (besides grass). I'd eat bikkies till I was full!

Most of all, I loved getting cuddles and "scritchy-scratchies" from Donna, and belly rubs from Phil. My favorite spot to hang out was on the rug in front of the wood-burning stove. I'd get so relaxed and snoozy that I'd nap belly-up.

It took my body four months to really get well, but it finally did. My fur grew in nice and shiny. I had a good appetite, and I gained weight fast. Donna started setting me down on the grass and dirt outside, to sniff and maybe even taste it. I've always been an excellent sniffer. I can tell when rain's coming, just by sniffing the air.

But my brain still had a long way to go. I was confused—was Donna my new mum? I knew I was getting too big to be sleeping in the house. When Donna sat down on the grass and I was supposed to be exploring next to her, I hid under her knees and peeked out. I liked being as close to my protector as possible.

"The outdoors" was a stranger ... and I was shy with strangers.

Donna gave me a huge stuffed elephant to cuddle and sleep with so that I might become less attached to her. I held on tight to that elephant and it got very scruffy, but I still followed Donna everywhere, and sometimes she would trip over me because I stayed so close to her feet. When she wasn't paying attention to me, I would bump her boots with my nose, hard. She called me her "Velcro wombat" or her "wee clinger." But little by little, every so often, I'd wander a short distance away, a tiny bit farther every time.

Slowly, I started going off and grazing on my own. I'd waddle over to one of the smaller, already-dug burrows, and I'd dig around at its entrance. Soon I was spending more time with my paws in the dirt than between Donna's feet.

Eventually, Donna moved me into a shed

I started to have a little fun.

behind their house. There was a dark box
for me to sleep in. My elephant came with
me, and there were some good logs to chew,
scratch, and rub myself on. Donna worried
about me. I cried plenty, but I was allowed
to go back and forth to the house, and I
became more independent.

Since then, I've been moving around

I still can't resist a tire.

between the shed, some different outdoor areas, the house, and primary school, which is a pen just outside the house, on a little hill.

Sorry, bub, I realize you didn't ask for my entire life story. I know it started sad, but it has gotten better and better. Anyway, here's a poem I wrote about my mum's pouch—practically all I remember from my old life. Maybe it will feel good to think about your mum's pouch.

My Mummy's Pouch
By Chance

I liked to ride inside my mummy's pouch.
Safe inside, nothing made me go "ouch!"
And I was happy with my mummy's pouch
. . . all around me.

I liked to look up at the sky and sniff the
   world out there.
The stars were twinkling up in the air.
And it smelled like my mummy was
   everywhere . . . all around me.

Wombat babies get to ride!
It's nice as it can be.
Mum's pouch was just right inside,
'Cause it was made for me.

45

As we both know all too well, humans do not have pouches (just one of the many differences between wombats and humans). I know their cloth pouches aren't the same as your mum's, but there are lots of different sizes to keep you perfectly snug and warm.

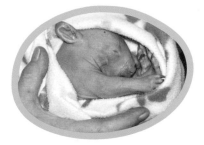

Elliot

Just some of the "teddy bears of the bush" that were raised here

Lucy

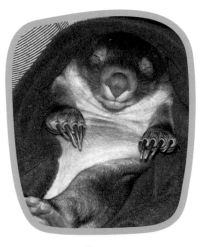

Barron

Some senior citizens in England sew and knit
them just for us. They read about Sleepy
Burrows online and wanted to help! If you
fuss enough when you're bigger, Donna might
wear your pouch over her shoulder and
carry you around the house all day. Whee!

Georgia

Abigail

Bundoo

Listen, bub. In my opinion, this is the most important thing for you to remember right now: You may be small, but you can still be the boss. Do not, under any circumstances, let the humans sleep. You are *made* to be up all night. You were *born* this way.

The humans are going to leave you alone most of the time now, as if you were still living quietly inside your mum's pouch. I'll leave you alone now, too, but I'll be back. Soon enough, you'll want to cuddle and play. Trust me, the humans will *not* be able to resist your charms. When I was small, even when I wouldn't let her sleep, Donna called me her "wee cuddle-bat."

Enjoy *every* snuggle, *buddy.* That's the wombat way.

CHAPTER 3
THE WOMBAT
WISHING STAR

Hey, I just heard Donna and Phil choose your name. Hi, Panzer!

"She needs a strong name," Donna said to Phil a few minutes ago. "Her body's so sturdy to have survived such a bad accident."

"Then let's name her Panzer," Phil suggested. "It's the German word for 'tank' or 'armor.'"

"Yes, exactly that!" Donna hooted. "Panzer!" And it was decided. Until now, they've been calling you "little bub," for the little baby you are.

I can hear you softly gulping down your milk and squealing for more. Donna measures the milk powder into our bottles, adds warm water, and shakes the bottle up. *Boom!* It has all the fat, protein, vitamins, and minerals we need. Bottles, pouches, sleeping, and staying warm are what nursery life is all about.

Donna's hands have touched every single wombat that has come through Sleepy Burrows.

Most pinkies need to eat every two hours. It's "pinky season" and there are just so *many* of you here these days, so Donna is serving up almost sixty bottles a day. She never misses one, though sometimes she has a volunteer, Cynthia, come to help. They have to be patient. Drinking a bottle can take awhile, because you'd only be getting a slow trickle of milk from your mum. And pinkies can get stressed out if they sense that their human caregiver is anxious; that's bad for your health.

Snort, slurp, snuffle, swallow, squeal, repeat. I hear pinkies make these feeding sounds a lot. They're the only sounds you guys really make. They're good, healthy sounds. They sound like life.

In a few months, Donna will give you your first tiny pile of carefully cut green grass.

Believe me, you'll be interested. She won't give you too much at a time, because that may make you poop a lot, as she's learned the hard way.

For now, though, Donna has to cover your eyes with a cloth so you don't get distracted when you drink. As you guzzle away, I can see your little nose, which—because it is so important—is pretty big already.

Besides getting fed, you'll get oiled. Mums' pouches naturally keep pinkies' skin healthy, but Donna has to do this with hemp oil every day. Her hands are strong and tough, but when she rubs oil onto the pinkies, her hands look like soft, gentle, magical butterflies.

Let me just tell you one more thing: The night I was rescued, Donna pointed out to Phil that

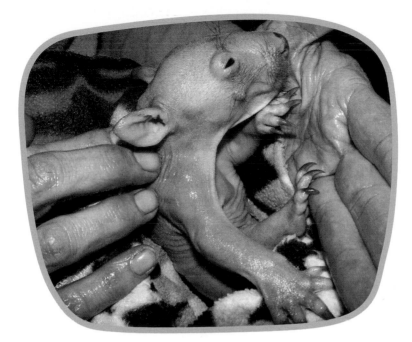

*Once you grow fur, you won't need
oil massages anymore!*

one star was twinkling the brightest. I made
a wish. What do you think I wished for?

Once you start going outside, you can make
wishes, too. Just relax now. I'll sing you a
lullaby, okay?

Twinkle, twinkle, little bub,
Stars shine in the sky above
Wombats wish upon a star . . .
Wonder what those wishes are?
Twinkle, twinkle, little bub,
Let's give you a belly rub!

Lullabies calmed Cruiser right down.

PART 2
RECOVERY
Creature Care

CHAPTER 4

LENDING A PAW

Donna and Phil are going to examine you. Luckily, I've followed you into the special-care area so we can continue our lessons. They're weighing you, looking for injuries, looking at your eyes, and taking your temperature by feeling your gums (they should be pink and slippery, and your mouth should be warm).

Donna may call Dr. Joseph for advice. He's come over in an emergency before, but usually they bring us to his office in Gundaroo, the nearest town. Hopefully you won't have to go, because it's not a short drive! Anyway, at exam time, you'll get 1,000 percent of Donna's attention. There's lots of medicine in a cabinet, like liquid antibiotics and eyedroppers for infections and a special bubble bath for skin diseases. There's olive oil for when we can't poop, and a hot-water bottle to keep us warm. Even though it isn't always pleasant to be treated, Donna uses everything she knows to help us.

It looks like the worst of your injuries is your bruising. Donna was worried that the accident had caused internal damage—wounds inside that you can't see. But you

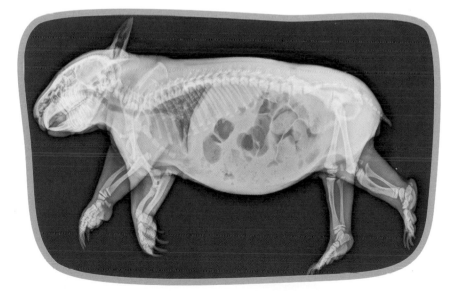

Dr. Joseph can see inside us!

don't show any signs of that. Your bruises look pretty bad, so Donna put herbal arnica oil on them. Humans use arnica on themselves, too, for bruises and bug bites.

Also, Donna can tell by your skin that you're dehydrated, so she'll get more fluids inside of you with small sips of warm water mixed with salt and sugar. And, of course, she'll keep feeding you and keeping you warm, because your body's too small to do that yourself. The thing is, you're so little. Many pinkies don't eat well enough, so they don't survive, or they get so stressed out that they just . . . I don't know . . . slip away.

Listen. If I can get big and strong, so can you. You didn't know me before—I used to be so small. And I was afraid of everything, even ants.

Getting weighed at the vet!

Donna's started your file, where she writes the facts of your rescue and records all your medical notes. She'll weigh you on a teeny-tiny scale every day and note your weight, so she can tell how fast you're growing and how much to feed you. You're supposed to gain 3 ½ ounces (100 g) each week—almost the weight of four slices of bread!

DONNA'S TO-DO LIST

Donna's a busy human. Every day, she:

- Plays and interacts with us for 5 to 7 hours
- Feeds us up to 60 bottles
- Finds and cuts 2 large bags of grass (in summer, this can take up to 3 hours a day)
- Distributes 17 pounds (8 kg) of sweet potatoes or carrots (depends on how much grass is found!) and 55 pounds (25 kg) of wombat granola
- Fills water bowls and waters trees (52 gallons [200 L] of water)
- Keeps the washer/dryer going from 9 a.m. to 5 p.m.
- Collects 2 buckets of our poop!

Donna has plenty of other work. She keeps records, does research, and raises money for the sanctuary.

Once I heard a human say that picking us up is like holding a dusty bowling ball with legs.

Hey, Panzer, by the time you stop growing, you could weigh almost 80 pounds (36 kg)!

Right now, your pouch—and Donna's arms—are your home. Soon enough, though, you'll start wombat kindergarten. You'll begin moving through the seven levels of wombat school here at Sleepy Burrows until you're back in the bush, bub! Here's how it works.

Most orphaned wombats go through the levels in order, but every wombat is different. Some of us start later, take longer in certain levels, or go back and forth. It depends on how healthy and confident we are.

1. The **Nursery** *(for pinkies up to 6 to 8 months)* is in the house. Here, pinkies eat, sleep, and stay warm. The tiniest stay in Donna's shirt for warmth. The bigger ones stay in pouches that hang from doorknobs in the quieter rooms of the house, like the office.

2. In **Kindergarten** *(for 8- to 12-month-olds)*, we're getting active and silly! We're still in the house, but we're moved to a separate room. We stay in crates (dog carriers, really) with hanging pouches inside, and we don't need to be held quite as much (though we still love it).

THE GREAT BEYOND!

Pens and burrows for elderly & disabled, or blind wombats.

THE GREAT BEYOND!

TO HORSE PADDOCK AND DAWN'S BURROW

DONNA & PHIL'S HOUSE

FIRST FIELD TRIPS HAPPEN HERE!

1 NURSERY

SHED

2 KINDERGARTEN

3 PRE-PRIMARY SCHOOL

HUMAN PARKING

GHOST GUM TREES

4 PRIMARY SCHOOL

TIRE PILE

6 HIGH SCHOOL

THE CREEK

5 MIDDLE SCHOOL

THE GREAT BEYOND!

7 BUSH UNIVERSITY

BRIDGE

½ MILE TO ROAD

EUCALYPTUS GROVE

GATES TO THE GREAT BEYOND!

3. **Pre-primary school** *(for 12-month-olds)* means we move from the pouched cages to "burrow boxes"—long, covered wood crates that feel like burrows. (A burrow is a lot like a pouch; it's dark and warm and it protects us.) In a burrow box, you can safely move around and explore, and there's a strong pouch hanging from a hook. We get lots of playtime inside the house . . . and we take field trips! On warm days we start going for short trips outside to sniff fresh air and explore grass, and dig a little in the dirt and rocks, all with Donna right there. Donna leaves us on the ground for longer and longer, like our real mums would, and lets us graze. Soon we don't need our pouches at all.

4. **Primary school** *(for 8- to 15-month-olds)* is made up of four pens on a fenced-in slope pretty close to the house. We learn

more about digging and grazing, and we're left alone more (our mums would have started leaving us for an hour or two each night). We still see Donna plenty, and most of us go back and forth from here to inside the house (especially if we're shy or clingy, like I was). We get our own burrows with sturdy tin roofs over the entrances, and there are logs, trees, rocks, and other natural "furniture" for us to climb over and dig under.

5. **Middle school** *(for 16- to 20-month-olds)* is three large pens located "up the back." It's a lot like primary school—we just see the humans less.

6. **High school** *(for 20- to 24-month-olds)* is in ten shelters located "up top." It's bigger than middle school and a little wilder, and we see the humans much less (they put

our food down when we're asleep). By now we've learned to protect ourselves and our burrows from other wombats. There's also lots of space for us to dig our own burrows, if we want.

High school "up top."

7. **Bush University** *(for 2-year-olds and up)*, located "way up top," is the last step. It's rare to see the humans there. There are

three huge pens with gates that open right into the wild.

There is also a shed for wombats with special needs. Wombats who are too big to live in burrow boxes—but aren't ready for primary school—stay there. Sick adult wombats might also stay there, because it's quiet and away from humans.

Oh, man, you're asleep again. Sorry, have I bored you? No problem, I'm just telling you *everything you need to know in life*. It's fine. I'll just go grumble and nip at the humans' legs so they know it's my carrot time, because they do seem to have forgotten.

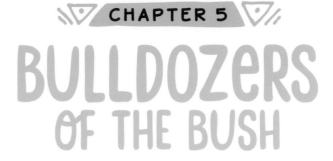

CHAPTER 5

BULLDOZERS OF THE BUSH

Hey, Panzer!

Wow! At five months old you now weigh two whole pounds and you're as big as an eggplant.

You're sleeping so much that I've barely seen you, and today is no different. I'm sorry to admit that it was getting a bit old watching you snooze, so I dug around in primary school for a day or so, and here I am, back to check on you as you hang from the doorknob. I can always smell my way right to you.

If you'd been awake, you'd have realized it's never an ordinary day around here. When

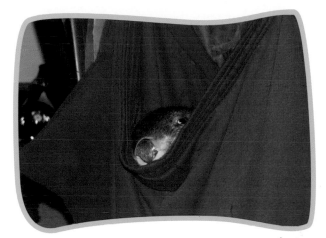

Sometimes there are so many pinkies that Donna runs out of dooknobs, and you have to hang from hooks on a wall!

I came in, Donna was on the phone with Dr. Joseph. When she hung up, she started crying in her weird human way. I know people think wombats make funny noises, but nothing sounds stranger than a human sobbing.

It took me some time to work out what was going on. I finally gathered that Abby the pinky had died. Neither Donna nor Dr. Joseph could figure out why, which drove them both crazy. Though she was small, Abby had been doing just fine. Until she wasn't.

Soon Donna wrapped Abby's little body in an old towel and put her in a shoebox. She was hardly any bigger than a baked potato. Donna took the box outside to bury her in the eucalyptus grove at the top of the hill, where she buries all wombats. I followed her. Donna has seen lots of pinkies like Abby "fade away," but she cries almost every time—sometimes a little, sometimes a lot.

After she had covered the hole with dirt, Donna closed her eyes and whispered the same thing she whispers to all joeys when she buries them: "Go dig hard in heaven with your real mum." Which might be the saddest sentence I've ever heard a human say.

Then, like she always does, Donna went into the shed and used a thick black permanent marker to write Abby's name on the "R.I.P." list. Next to that, there's a long list of all the wombats Donna's released. It helps remind her of all the happy endings.

I stayed right under Donna's feet as she headed back inside. She had to dance and hop a bit so she wouldn't trip. Inside, she put her elbows on the kitchen counter and leaned over with her head in her hands. Then she sighed deeply, walked to the sink, washed her hands, splashed her face, put on the electric kettle for more coffee, smeared honey on a crumpet, ate it fast, and started preparing bottles, including yours.

If you keep up all this good bottle work, you'll get bigger and stronger fast. Your

body is already amazing, though. Just look at your huge claws—those are some sharp little shovels. That's why we're called the "bulldozers of the bush." Built to dig, baby!

Abby had been one of the tiniest pinkies Donna had saved.

Haven't you slept long enough, mate? Open your eyes and check me out—don't you want to see what you'll look like? We have four long, strong teeth in front, plus three molars on each side—top and bottom. Our front teeth never stop growing. We wear them down by gnawing on grass, roots, and rocks (I know that sounds strange, but rocks keep us healthy). CHOMP!

Also, we have *very* powerful bums, or butts! And if you are unlucky enough to get a "bum-buck," you get whacked hard by another wombat's butt!

Hey, they didn't name you Panzer for nothin'. So slurp, gulp, guzzle, and swallow away. Before you know it, your body will be ready to do what it's made to do.

The famous wombat smile! We say hello to humans with a nice hard nip.

Our heads are flat and broad. Males' heads usually get wider and flatter as we grow; females' stay a little pointier.

Our eyes are tiny to keep out dust.

Our ears are tiny (but joeys' ears look ridiculously big).

Our nostrils are huge. Smelling is the way we understand the world. We are outstanding sniffers. It's like we have smell-o-vision.

Our backs have super-strong muscles.

Our bums are flat and bony, with an extra-thick layer of skin.

Our tails are small and stubby, so a predator (like a fox or dingo) can't grab on and drag us out of our burrows.

Our legs are short and powerful.

CHAPTER 6
DiRT PaLaCES

Your teeth are coming in, Panzer—that means fewer bottles and more solid food! You're already six months old! You weigh three pounds and you're as big as a pineapple—without the leaves. *Sniff, sniff*—little bub's growing up! You're getting your fuzz, too—you're no pinky anymore. Your fur is just a shadow of what it will become, but you're becoming a velvet. And . . . you've graduated from the nursery to kindergarten!

Aww. I see you've become an older buddy to not one but two newcomer pinkies, Lincoln and Barron. I've taught you well.

Do you want a sneak peek of what you'll be learning in school? I don't think it's ever too early to learn about burrows.

You and your new buddy, Lincoln. He's named after a war tank, just like you are.

Burrows are like long, underground dirt palaces. We dig these tunnels ourselves, but when you and I go bush (return to the wild), we'll probably just find ones that have already been dug. A burrow might be up to ten feet (3 m) deep and one hundred feet (30 m) long! I can't wait to have a real burrow of my own. Some wombats use up to ten different ones,

Every wombat has a favorite burrow.

but I'd be happy with just one, if it was all mine.

Most burrows have a cozy "bedroom"—a hollow of dry dirt or dust and maybe a little bed made of grass. If Donna or Phil crawled

way, way, way into a wombat's burrow (which
they might have, knowing them), they would
find areas big enough for them to sit up in!
Burrows keep us cool in summer and warm
in winter, just like human houses do for the
humans.

What does a wombat do in a burrow? We
sleep. Above ground, we can sleep standing
up! But in the burrow, rest gets serious.

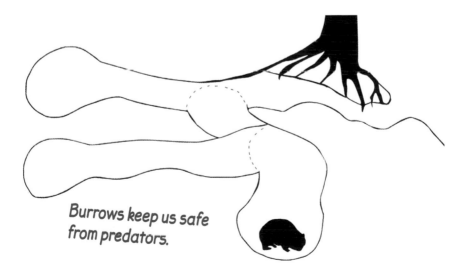

Burrows keep us safe
from predators.

First, we snooze on our sides or bellies. Then we roll over onto our backs, belly up, legs straight up in the air. Sweet dreams! If we're sleeping really hard, it can be impossible to wake us up! If it's cold, we might curl up in a ball, like a cat. We shuffle out of our burrows at dusk to start grazing, which we continue all night long.

Some burrows have been around a hundred years, and most have been lived in by a bunch of different wombats! We like to fix them up for ourselves and change things around, though. When humans do this, they call it "home renovation."

Burrows are great places for being alone. You are going to need a good burrow.

Remember to take a **time-out** when you **need** one, Panzer. That's the **wombat way.**

CHAPTER 7

VELVET PLAYTIME

It was kind of a big day around here, Panzer. Look!

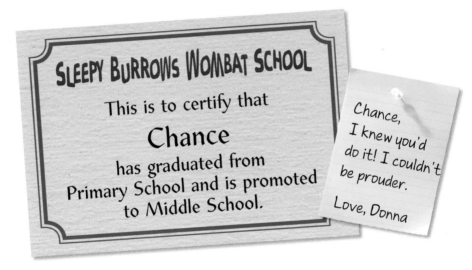

SLEEPY BURROWS WOMBAT SCHOOL

This is to certify that

Chance

has graduated from Primary School and is promoted to Middle School.

Chance,
I knew you'd do it! I couldn't be prouder.

Love, Donna

I know you haven't seen much of me. Donna usually lets me come and go around human dinnertime, and I sniff around the porch a good bit. I hardly ever come inside anymore, so I've missed seeing you. I *have* been peeking in, and I see you're a true velvet now.

You're seven months old, five pounds, and as big as a bag of sugar. Being a velvet means the living room is your personal playground. Let the games begin!

You're racing around in circles every afternoon when you get your burst of energy. Wrestle, wriggle! Zig, zag! Zip, zoom!

A pinky turning into a velvet!

Bounce, pounce! Also, roll and tumble! Tug and tear! Hop and skip! Did I forget anything?

I'm happy you have some good buddies your age. Play is important—it's how you learn, and it's how you get strong and smart enough to live in the bush. Grown-up wombats like to be alone (I've been feeling that way more and more). But you kids still love to be silly with one another and the humans. Velvet silliness is special!

I see you're coming out of your pouch more, like Cruiser.

Take silliness seriously, Panzer. That's the wombat way.

But! You're still *sooo* clingy, bub! (Hey, no judgment, I realize I was ever so slightly clingy myself.) If you can't see Donna and there's, say, a couch between you, and you can't climb around it or under it, you'll just try to climb right over it. Then you're stuck way up there, aren't you? You could fall and break a bone, so Donna supervises you carefully, like you're a human toddler. Roaming free is for later.

I see you've all discovered the joy of ramming into Donna with your head—hard! That woman is really very patient. If another wombat kept headbutting me, even if he was a cute, sweet little velvet, I'd turn around and bite his bum!

11 CLASSIC VELVET MOVES

Donna knows that when those big ears are down, you are either cranky or it's cuckoo time! Make sure you and your goofy mates try all of these popular activities:

Cruiser loves laundry time.

Bungi's favorite toy is shoelaces.

- **Sprint, Stop & Turn:** Run at top speed, stop suddenly, turn completely around, and repeat. Variation: Instead of stopping, go straight into a somersault.

- **The Grab & Drag:** Have your way with blankets and pillows that are meant to stay on the couch.

- **Head Boink:** Lift and jerk your nose up in the air. Repeat one hundred times.

Velvet Popcorn: Jump into the air, onto the couch, or onto other objects or people (such as Donna). This move is also commonly known as the Boing-Boing.

 The Head Toss: Swing your head like crazy side to side, feeling the wildness in every part of your body.

Nipping & Yipping: This is the reason Donna is used to bruises, even though she wears "wombat armor": heavy pants or jeans and boots.

Bungi could have won a gold medal in nipping and yipping.

- **Carpet Digging:** This one needs no explanation. Highly recommended.
- **Going Flat:** Lie very flat on your belly and smile proudly, showing your teeth.
- **Air Bum:** Stick your bum up and wag it around.
- **Velvet Piggyback:** Jump onto another velvet's back and hang on as long as you can.
- **Playing Dead:** Roll onto your back, legs sticking up, and become completely still for five seconds, until you start all your wacko moves all over again.

Donna calls lots of the velvets "tickle-bats."

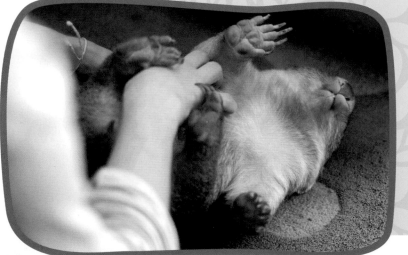

You know, watching you play kind of makes me miss my toys. I'd still like to have some. I do happen to have a list handy, if it ever occurs to Donna and Phil to ask:

Chance's Wish List

✓ 100 pillowcases and blankets in different colors

✓ one good burlap sack that smells strongly of oats

✓ as many shoelaces as possible

✓ at least one couch cushion I am allowed to chew on

✓ four new soccer balls

✓ a tire that is all mine (no other wombat's smells on it!)

Anyway, I know it's not all fun and games lately. Some things are new and scary, like going outside on mini-adventures.

The first few times you went outside, I saw you stay in your pouch and poke your nose out to sniff the air. When Donna put you on the grass, you kind of freaked out, and you nosed your pouch until Donna put you back in. Then you hid your head. Now you seem more confident wandering around for a few minutes at a time, but you're always happy to be tucked back in. That makes sense. It's how you would be acting with your mum.

But no doubt . . . inside the house, you're getting sassy for sure, mate!

When you get a little bigger, around the time you would have left your mum's pouch for good, Donna will start taking you on *real* bush

I loved finding fresh grass on my bush walks.

walks. These hikes are like little tours of your future! Donna will stay close, as your mum would have, but she'll take you around as much land as she can, so you'll have a map of the area in your head and can be ready to choose a burrow later.

You have to try to keep up with her. But sometimes these walks get too long for

a little one, and Donna will have to carry you back home. Thanks to us, she is a very strong woman.

How my first bush walk ended.

Oh, Panzer, I've been away so much I didn't realize you had officially moved up a level—I just heard Donna proudly tell the volunteer Monica that you've graduated from kindergarten. Congratulations. Are you ready for some serious dirt?

PART 3
REHABILITATION
School Days

CHAPTER 8

SCHOOL SUPPLIES

Sorry I slept through one of your first important afternoons in school. I was kind of exhausted because I was playing rough with an old tire of Phil's. It's a long story. Things got a little out of hand. Everything is fine now.

You're sleeping pretty hard in your burrow box. Donna just peeked in on you and chuckled. At eight months, you're as big as a sack of potatoes.

You had a long "Dirt and Rocks for Beginners" lesson today, didn't you? Well, spring is a great time to take this class. I was a very fast learner in this area. Truly, dirt is so delightful that I need to share some details.

You'll also use dirt for dust baths. I got an easy

A+ in this class. Believe it or not, dust baths are perfect for cleaning your fur and protecting your skin from sunburn. They also get rid of

The Low-Down on Dirt
By Chance

Why is dirt awesome? You can count the reasons on one muddy paw.

1. It's great to gobble because it has important nutrients that keep you healthy. That's just a wombat thing.

2. Whether you're happy, angry, sad, or bored, digging in dirt feels good. It feels great between your claws.

3. By digging, you can tell other wombats, "Stay away, this is my territory. Mind your own business!"

4. When it rains, dirt turns to mud. Marvelous mud!

5. Fresh dirt smells good.

So why does Donna keep trying to clean it out from under her fingernails? Just another weird human thing, I guess.

ticks and mites (mites are tiny bugs that cause mange, a horrible and deadly skin disease I refuse to discuss). By the way, we never groom ourselves the way cats do, and we rarely agree to baths in water, like dogs might. To clean our fur, we just scratch off the dirt. We're good scratchers, and we'll also rub against rocks, logs, or trees. In fact, there's a rock outside the house that's shiny because so many wombats have scratched themselves against it.

Here's how you take a dust bath: First, lie on dusty, *not muddy*, ground. Use your front paws to scoop and throw that delightful dirt over your whole body! Wriggle around on your back and belly—oh joy! Senior wombats especially love dust bathing.

Say **yes** to the **mess,** Panzer.
That's the **wombat way.**

Look at this muddy bundle.

CHAPTER 9

GLORIOUS GRASS

I see you're continuing to work hard, bub. You're nine months old now, and the size of a one-year-old human baby! You may *want* to graduate as fast as you can, and that's great, but remember, you're only ready when you're ready.

Anyway, no one can be released when there's this much rain. The risk of flash flooding is just too high. If you're asleep in your burrow when water rushes in, well, I don't need to explain what happens. If you're out and about, you'll have no burrow to go back to. Wombats fight over the burrows that aren't flooded and all your grass gets washed away.

We may be stubborn, but so is Mother Nature. Donna is stubborn, too, but she has to wait out storms like any other creature. In the rainy season, our world becomes Planet Mud. Humans' boots, socks, raincoats, and pants get so muddy when they're out there pumping out our flooded burrows, they don't even bring them inside. They just leave everything out on the deck, and nothing seems to ever get dry.

Floods can happen any time of year.

At some point, hungry, old, injured, or sick wombats waddle back to the feeding station, looking like huge heaps of furry chocolate pudding. Donna might bring them inside, and that's when she officially loses her battle against the mud.

Floods are tough, but once things dry out a bit, it's a great time to dig new burrows and hollow out and fix up old ones. And grass will grow soon. The grass after floods is so green it practically glows. It's a perfect time for release.

Oh, gee, now you're whining. Do you miss your bottle, Panzer? Well, luckily Donna is still gathering fresh cut-up grass just for you and your velvet mates every day.

Glorious, gorgeous grass! Donna tosses bright, beautiful piles right on the kitchen floor. The piles look like emerald pyramids. In the bush, we spend up to eight hours every day looking for good grass and then gobbling it up.

Would you like to know the best kinds of grass? That's easy. Golden beard grass,

Gobble-icious grass, all for Silo.

black spear grass, sword grass, bottle-washer grass, three-awn grass, wallaby grass, kangaroo grass, Mitchell grass, tussock (grass bunch), and scrubby bush like bluebush. What's my favorite?

Donna still wants you to gobble up lots of your other food so you're fattened up before you go bush.

Impossible to choose, really. But not all kinds grow all year, and if there's not enough rain, that's a situation.

Grass is always our plan A. But when there's no grass, we'll happily go right to plan B: bark, roots, shrubs, moss, rocks, and tiny sticks. Food stays in our bodies for up to two weeks (humans' bodies only hold food for a few days), and our bodies make the most of what we find.

Wanna know what else? Our poop is cube-shaped. There's a really good reason. We poop near our burrows to let others know they're in our territory. The burrow entrances can be steep and rocky, so our square poop won't roll away. Also, we can leave one hundred little pieces of poop a night.

Gee, Panzer, what would you do without me here to teach you things?

CHAPTER 10

CREATURE CLASSES

Happy first birthday! You've graduated to primary school! I'm so happy for you.

You may not be thinking about this yet, but I sure am.

GRADUATION REQUIREMENTS

In order to be safely released, you must:

 Be at least two years old and weigh at least 55 pounds (25 kg). If you're lighter than that, you can't protect yourself.

 Be used to living outside in all kinds of weather (storms, rain, and the hottest and coldest temperatures).

Know how to forage (find your own food).

Be afraid of dingoes, foxes, dogs, and humans. (Not all humans are like Donna and Phil; you can't waddle up to just any of them. And you should be terrified of any dog except for Stella and Bella.)

Speaking of graduation requirements, I should tell you the facts of fighting. It's not pleasant to think about, but it's part of bush life.

Soldier is the biggest, toughest wombat Donna has ever raised.

WOMBAT COMBAT

We only fight for important reasons:

 We need (or want) our feeding area all to ourselves. We may also fight another wombat for its territory because we don't have enough grass in ours, like when there is a drought (not enough rain).

 We have to tell another wombat that our burrow is ours, not theirs. Only one wombat (plus a joey) at a time can stay in each burrow.

 Females must protect their joeys (watch out when that's the case, seriously).

 Males will fight each other for girlfriends.

We hardly ever kill each other during an attack, but a fight is always serious. If we're badly hurt or left burrowless, we may die from infections or extreme heat or cold. Too much heat or light can kill us, even if we're not injured already.

When we're scared, we might run into a burrow or a hollow log. When we're angry or threatened, we might growl, sway our head, hiss, or bare our teeth.

When two large, angry males fight, Donna calls it "going full bull." Our strength and determination allow us to battle hard and long. We can ram into each other's heads straight on. If we're grabbed from behind, we can kick backward with our back legs, like donkeys.

We can also bite the other wombat's ear or side and do some real damage. Some of us have major scars on our bodies. But females tend to scream and use their size to scare others off, to avoid fighting.

Fights can get serious.

Sorry if I scared you, Panzer. I was trying to motivate you. You don't have to fight anytime soon.

This was my schedule in kindergarten and primary school:

Daytime
- Dirt play
- Burrow lessons (slowly exploring "practice" burrows of all sizes that other wombats have dug)
- Snack (grass from a patch that Donna brings us to, plus carrots and wheat biscuits)
- Peekaboo with burlap sack
- Tug-of-war with ropes and old shirts, with Donna (a major strength-builder)
- Many very long naps throughout

Nighttime (advanced wombats only!)
- Foraging
- Free play with dirt (mud if it rains!)
- Rock chewing
- Intermediate burrow digging (making tunnels longer, adding new openings to existing burrows)

Listen, Panzer, I'm sorry to lecture you
about this. But I think you should maybe
try to concentrate a little harder with your
burrow work. You seem a little scattered
when you dig. You look like you're daydreaming.
It's not enough to just poke your nose into
the practice burrow; you're supposed to
keep going until you hit a dead end.

It's okay, I know it's new to you. You'll keep
getting different burrowy things to practice
crawling into and sitting in, to get the feel
of being in the tunnels. In the wild, we would
have started digging our own practice
burrows when we were only eight months old
(though we would have still slept in our mum's
burrow). In some pens, Donna and Phil have
built burrows from a plastic or concrete tube in
their thoughtful human way.

But eventually, most of us will have to use the

I used a tunnel
made from old tires.

Ruth and Parcel
had a plastic tube

Some wombats lay upside
down in their practice burrows.

real deal. Usually, we just need to decide if
a certain empty burrow is good enough for
us. But even a fixer-upper involves plenty of
digging. It may need to be cleaned out because

BURROW BASICS

1. **Look for the perfect place.** Head straight for the slopes at the creek banks and check out your possibilities. The dirt there is like muddy clay. Rocks or tree roots around the entrance are bonuses, so your burrow won't collapse too quickly in a flood.

2. **Use your front paws and claws to loosen the dirt.** Then scoop away! Back away from the hole bit by bit, using your back legs to push the dirt away. You can even move dirt with your nose! Before you know it, it'll be tunnel time.

3. **Dig and dig and dig some more.** Dig until your tunnel is very long. Longer than you ever imagined . . . you might even be able to dig for 100 feet (30 m).

4. **Remember: SAFETY FIRST.** Keep the entrance narrow to protect yourself from predators. If you can, add another opening so you can escape, especially from floods. Always good to have options.

5. **Make a bedroom.** Bring in some soft ferns or tussocks to make yourself a comfy bed. A good day's sleep is important.

6. **Don't forget to poop at the entrance.** You want other wombats to stay out.

parts of it have collapsed, its openings may need to be repaired, or it may need more room inside. If you're going to start from scratch, here's the deal:

Once you're set up, you'll get into a routine. Obviously, you'll sleep there all day. When you come out in the late afternoon, you'll move slowly and sniff the air at the entrance to see who may be around. You'll sit in your "lie patch" just outside the burrow opening—it's a mound of

It took Peanut awhile to learn what a burrow was ... and wasn't.

soft dirt that you've moved from inside the burrow, like a little front porch. Here you can lie down and catch the last rays of sun. You can even take a mini-nap.

Create a **home** you **love,** Panzer. That's the **wombat way.**

As I've mentioned, our burrows, and our bodies, really protect us out there in the bush.

You already know that our bums have built-in armor. It's no joke. Our backsides are made of four bone plates covered in tough cartilage, fat, thick skin, and fur. The whole thing is called a "dermal shield" ("dermal" means "skin"). Dingoes, dogs, and foxes can claw and bite at our bums all they want, but they can't really hurt us.

Sometimes a predator decides it would be a good idea to attack our burrow. So we back right up to the entrance, bum first, and just wait it out. We can stand there all day and night—who could ever get past that rump?

If the predator makes the regrettable decision to try to wedge its pointy little head in anyway, we really have no choice. Our next move quickly ends the attack.

Are you ready to know about the move? Think carefully. Once you know this, you can't *unknow* it. Yes? Okay.

We use our bums to smoosh their head right up against the wall of our burrow!

I am completely serious about this. I can feel my bum becoming strong enough to do it, if I am forced to.

CHAPTER 11

TURNING WILD?

February

AGE: 15 months

WEIGHT: 40 pounds (18 kg)

AS BIG AS: an adult's rolled-up sleeping bag

Something kind of bad and weird happened yesterday afternoon, Panzer. Now that you're bigger and more mature, I'd like to tell you about it. You're a great listener, and maybe someday you'll even start yipping back. I'm slightly curious about what's happening in that furry head of yours.

I was in my spot near the wood stove, near the log that we all love to chew, claw, and rub up against. It was velvet crazy time, and a few velvets were doing their popcorn routine on and off the couch. "Sofa-bats!" Donna kept chuckling. (She used to call me a sofa-bat, too, but she's stopped letting me up there because my paws are too dirty now.)

Donna kept giggling and playing tug-of-war with them. All of a sudden I noticed that the wall behind the couch smelled good. Like, *really* good. That was because the walls are made of drywall, which is made from rocks that have been turned into a powdery material. And as I've mentioned, we eat rocks. The urge to gnaw overwhelmed me. I waddled over, squeezed behind the couch, and made a tiny little nick with my largest, strongest front tooth. I was surprised by how easy it was to dig into that drywall and chomp away. I really got into the rhythm of it. I used my whole body—I felt so strong! I must have looked crazy.

And because I was behind the couch, Donna couldn't see me! Soon the hole was the size of a football.

I'm sure you saw this coming, but eventually, Donna heard my gnawing and gnashing. She yelled, "OH NO, CHANCE!" Then she waved a big couch cushion to move me away from the wall, and she used her foot to gently shove me to the door, all the while saying in a singsongy voice, "Okay, wild boy! Okay, wild wombat! About time to find your own rocks outside, isn't it? Go find some, there are lots. You'll know what to do, wild boy. Little by little."

No one has ever called me "wild" before. People have used many other words to describe me, mostly these: "*Rescued.*" "*Orphaned.*" "*Injured.*" "*Poor little thing.*" "*Sweet.*"

I've also been called "*lucky*," "*chatter-bat*," "*cuddle-bat*," "*sofa-bat*," "*tickle-bat*," and "*mud-bat*." Of course, they've also said I'm strong and smart. But they've never, ever said "wild."

Wild boy, Donna had said. *Wild wombat*. I heard it clear as a bell. She'd said "wild" three times.

Soon Donna had moved me all the way to the sliding glass door and was using her foot to shove me out. Before I even knew what I was doing, I gave her leg a good chomp. I'd never done such a thing. Donna yelped loudly and continued to shove me out, closing the sliding glass door between us fast so that I couldn't get back in.

Just like that, I was outside and she was in. I didn't like how she had just treated me. It

seemed really rude, forcing me out that way.
I considered throwing a tantrum.

I looked around. I noticed it had rained
earlier. I waddled down the stairs from
the porch to the nearest grassy, rocky
area and started to grind on some of the
rocks there. They didn't taste quite as good
as the wall, and they didn't feel nice and
smooth in my mouth.

I walked back to the sliding glass door.
Donna was calmly cleaning and bandaging
her leg as the velvets continued their
popcorn routine. She glanced at me, but
ignored me. I growled. No response. I whined.
Still nothing.

The next logical step was chewing hard on
the wooden door frame. Major success!
Once I'd done enough damage to the frame,

I was able to knock the huge screen out.
It clanged loudly on the porch and Donna
looked up again. I stamped and stomped so
that the screen tore and the metal got good
and dented. *You're not the boss of me, Donna.*

But nothing changed, not at all. I was not
going to be allowed back inside.

Soon Donna came out and opened the shed
door. She seemed very calm. I ignored her
but I shuffled right in. I was relieved to see
my elephant, and I curled up next to him.
I slept, even though it was nighttime. The
whole ordeal had taken a lot out of me. I
really wanted biscuits.

But I slept badly. I had a nightmare that
Donna hadn't ever come outside to make
sure I got into the shed safely. In the dream,
something that I can only describe as a

giant mud beast was lumbering slowly straight toward me. It was a wombat I'd never seen before. It stopped about twenty feet away and gave a low growl. Even though I knew I should stand still and growl back, I turned and ran. I hid in a burrow under the house. I could hear Donna and Phil walking around above me. I stayed there, but I just wanted to be aboveground—and inside. I didn't belong outside or down here. I promised myself that if I could just be back in the house, I would play more gently and stay away from that wall.

The mud beast.

In my nightmare, I remembered that there have been fights in that burrow. I've heard them. First it sounds like a car has rammed into the one end of the house. The floor vibrates. You can hear the bashing and banging of pipes and wombat versus wombat. Donna and Phil would prefer it if the burrow did not exist, because they can't help wombats if they're fighting and someone's getting hurt. The humans will pour concrete down it (when it's empty, of course), but we always find a way to dig around it.

I was relieved to wake up and be in the shed, where I smelled Donna and felt bright light pouring in. She was standing in the doorway. "Chance spent the night in the shed," she called out to Phil. "I think this wombat is finally turning wild. Last night he chewed a hole in the wall, then he bit me!"

"Hmm," Phil said. "I assume the door frame and the screen are also courtesy of our darling Chance?"

"You got that right," Donna laughed. Then I saw the bandage on her leg. Whoops. Things did turn pretty wild last night, and it was all my doing.

For the record, I hadn't meant to hurt Donna. She's been very good to me.

Then things seemed totally back to normal. The humans seemed proud of me. I stayed up all day, which I haven't done since I was stuck in that bathtub, and followed Donna around, munching grass as she cut some for you guys.

Thanks for listening, bub. I suppose this is a perfect time to share with you the rules of wombattitude, which I understand now better than ever.

WOMBATTITUDE

To be a happy wombat in the wild, you've got to remember these four things.

With wombattitude, the sky's the limit.

1. **Work with what makes you weird.** Some humans think we're shaped funny and we move awkwardly. They laugh about how we eat rocks, how we use our bums, and how our legs look too short for our bodies. And they think we're lazy. But hey—we're practically made of muscle, our bums protect us, and we can use our legs to run really fast when we need to. Plus, "lazy" can also be thought of as "saving up energy for when you need it."

2. **Don't apologize for being yourself.** When I bit Donna, I was just being a normal wombat. She knew that.

3. **Keep plowing through.** Face what comes your way straight on. Dig in your heels. Be stubborn. You want something? Insist on it—don't stop until you get it. Stand your ground. (But stay alert so you keep safe.)

Move headfirst through any obstacle in your path.

4. **Prove 'em wrong.** Sometimes Donna is sure that a certain wombat can't be released, and she plans for him or her to stay on as a permanent resident. But later, she's surprised and happy to discover she was wrong. If anyone understands how tough we are, it's Donna. But humans can't know everything, and even Donna can underestimate our "push for the bush."

Once you fully gain your wombattitude, everything is different.

Screeching's a big part
of wombattitude.

RELEASE

Graduation

CHAPTER 12
SANCTUARY STARS

I bet you're wondering when—and if—all this hard work will pay off and you'll be "bush ready." I've overheard plenty on the topic. If you haven't realized, not all of us make it back to the bush. Some wombats just can't survive out there. They stay in pens close to the house; they are protected and have everything they need. Like, Robby's broken hip never healed right, so she can't really dig. And Devika will always be too small to live in the bush. She was born with a split in her tongue, so she never got enough milk from her mum as a pinky.

The permanent residents have an important job: They're teachers. Kids and adults visit to learn about the marsupials with whom they share their land, and they see the permanent wombats (the rest of us shouldn't get too used to humans). The visitors hear all of our stories, even the saddest ones. People around the world see them online. The more people learn about our situations, the more they will think about driving carefully, checking for wombats on the side of the road, and figuring out ways to live peacefully alongside all wildlife.

For most of us, though, "silly and sweet" eventually becomes "stubborn and sturdy." Little by little, being powerful and getting our way becomes top priority, and the humans plan for our

Elderly Dawn stayed safe in a pen and enjoyed chewing shoes.

release. You know this by now; remember my little wall incident.

Of course, you *could* get tickles and biscuits from Donna and Phil for a long time. But that's not the goal.

Soon you'll want to spend most of your time in primary school, so you'll come back to the

Wild creatures need wild spaces.

Stay *stubborn*, Panzer. That's the *wombat way*.

house less often. And as you move up the levels, you'll miss the humans less and less. Donna and Phil call this "the soft release process." I think of it as "my great adventure."

At the end of the journey, Donna and Phil just leave the gate of Bush University open, and whenever you're ready, you can walk right out. There's a camera so they can see which direction you went. You can even come and go, if you need to. I may do that myself, in case I change my mind. But basically, when you stay out for at least a few days at a time, you've graduated! From then on, you're called a Sanctuary Star.

Here are some Sanctuary Stars I've known

personally. A few of them even bit my bum. I'm so happy for them! I guess these guys all wished upon the Wombat Wishing Star:

Pecan the expert back scratcher.

Another toughie, Silo.

The humans adore me. What's that, Panzer?
Aw, thanks, I know you do, too. But Donna
needs the space (and the time and energy!) to
help more wombats. So now it's about time for
me to move to high school. Maybe you'll be able
to visit me a few times; just have Donna walk
you to the fence when she takes you on a bush
walk. Then stand there till I smell you.
Okay?

Clipper the bush boy.

Veg and her daughter.

Find your wild space and live there,
Panzer. That's the wombat way.

CHAPTER 13

ONE STEP CLOSER

Oh, Panzer! I'm so glad you could visit me. I'd been hoping Donna would include the "up top" area in your bush walks. I was afraid I'd never smell you again.

Lookit! This burrow was here when I arrived, and it was huge, but I've really improved it. I cleaned out all the sticks and leaves. The first time I went way down into it, I fell asleep and didn't come out for almost thirty-six hours. The humans got worried about me!

And do you know my neighbor, Penelope? Her burrow is over there. We were velvets together inside. We get along fine, but we pretty much leave each other alone, like we will in the wild someday soon.

Let's see, what else can I show you? Okay, here. I dug and dug in this spot until I hit this tree root. It turns out it's delicious, so I gnaw on it as soon as I wake up. I'll leave some for you, for when it's your turn here. After all, you *were* the last friend I made at Sleepy Burrows.

Listen, Panzer. We need to talk.

One day very soon, you won't see me here. Right, I thought that would get your attention. It's because I'll have graduated to Bush University.

I know it's about to happen, because last night I sent a rather strong message to the humans. I tried to dig under the fence to get out. But Phil's kind of a genius with the concrete and he outsmarted me with the foundation. I think I damaged the fence, though.

See, I can't be contained anymore. All of my muscles are humming and thrumming to bust me out. I have to be *out there*. I have to say goodbye. Did you know I'm already three years old?

Oh, Panzer! If your mum could see you now, she'd be so proud. Bye, brave little mate. Good luck.

And, of course, *yip, yip, yip*. Only us wombats know what *that* means.

There really is no other creature just like us, don't you agree? And there's no other wombat just like *you*, Panzer.

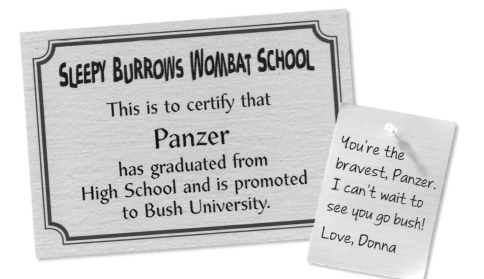

SLEEPY BURROWS WOMBAT SCHOOL

This is to certify that

Panzer

has graduated from
High School and is promoted
to Bush University.

You're the bravest, Panzer. I can't wait to see you go bush!

Love, Donna

CHAPTER 14

WILD BOY

I've been thinking of you a lot. You don't hear me going *yip, yip, yip* anymore, do you? It's because . . . guess what . . . I made it! I'm so far out in the bush, I can see the Great Beyond through the fence!

What did the humans do a few nights ago when they discovered that I had waddled casually through the open gate and left the pen up top? Maybe they felt happy and sad at the same time. I felt the same way, for sure. But mostly I felt wild and ready.

Living in the wild is better than I imagined. It's like a new planet. There's a kind of eucalyptus tree out here that I'd never smelled, and its roots are delicious. I love feeling fresh earth beneath my paws all the

SLEEPY BURROWS WOMBAT SCHOOL

This is to certify that

Chance

has graduated from Bush University and has moved into his future as a truly wild wombat.

Be free, my lovely boy. I'll always be here if you need me.

Love, Donna

time, dirt I don't have to share with other wombats.

Every day, I feel less like a teddy bear of the bush and more like a tough bear of the bush. I know you've probably always thought of me as *tough*. Just between us, I was faking it a little, trying to encourage you. Or maybe I was trying to encourage myself. "Fake it till you make it," the humans say!

I found an empty burrow deep in a eucalyptus grove and fixed it up. I'm sleeping incredibly well here, as well as I did in my mum's pouch. I made it my home. I created a good lie patch—great for spacing out before I start my nightlife of searching for good grass, which has been hard work. You've probably noticed there hasn't been a drop of rain. The grass isn't as green and delicious as it should be, and there's never any dew on it. So as I search for grass, I just keep telling myself, *Wild, wild. I'm a wild boy.*

Well, I can always sniff my way back to the feeding station to fill my belly. If the humans see me at the station, I bet they'll get excited, but they'll keep their distance unless I seem sick or hurt. And Stella will check up on me, too.

In any case, when I'm near the house, I plan to sniff around and peek in on you. Maybe you'll be in high school soon. I'll stand on the other side of the fence and go *yip, yip, yip*, and you'll respond, because you're big enough to *yip* now, too. Then we can have a little visit, like we used to.

I hope you'll go wild soon after that. I hope I see you out here in the bush. I'll give you a nice friendly nip.

You'll love it out here, Panzer. It's so quiet at night, you can almost hear the millions of stars twinkling.

As a matter of fact, the Wombat Wishing Star is twinkling really brightly tonight, like it's flashing on and off. I'm going to wish for rain. Just the right amount though—not too much!

You should make a wish, too.

LUCKY STARS

BY PANZER

Well, you've heard plenty from Chance, haven't you? He thinks he knows everything, and he kind of does, doesn't he? But I know a fair bit now, too. Thanks to Chance, Donna, and Phil, and because of my wild instincts, things turned out pretty great for me. Things turned out pretty great for Chance, too.

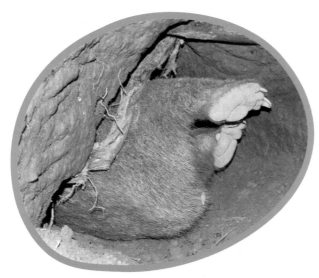

Toward the end, all the humans saw of Chance was his bum sticking out of his burrow!

Soon after his first walk into the wild, Chance started coming back to Bush University off and on. A huge male, Soldier, had also been released out there, and Donna thought perhaps he had threatened Chance. So a neighbor, Beth, offered to take Chance onto her property, because the big male on her land had just died.

Whenever Beth spots Chance she reports back to Donna, who can't stop smiling about the news—he's even bigger than he was when he first graduated. He's bulked up with muscle from all his digging! Donna thinks he must weigh seventy-seven pounds (35 kg) by now.

Chance has moved out of his first burrow, and the location of his new one is a mystery. He still visits the old one and leaves poop sometimes, as if to say "this one is still mine!" Beth sees him once in a while, after he's

visited a dam near her house. He shuffles around happily in thick, giant puffs of herbs called lomandra.

And now Chance is a daddy—twice! *Yip, yip, yip.*

I went bush in October, nine months after Chance did. It felt easy. I found a sweet little burrow by the creek, near a grove of dark, scruffy-barked eucalyptus with good thick roots, and I made it my own. It has a solid entrance and it looks like it has stayed safe through many floods. I'm going to make it even bigger, with a new bedroom. As I graze all night long, the frogs in the creek sing their spring song.

I'm pretty sure I smelled my "baby brother" Barron recently, when I was out foraging. I hope I run into him at the feeding station sometime. Lincoln, too. Love those little fellas!

The bush was a great place to celebrate my third birthday.

So far I've had no major problems, but last night, just for fun, I wandered over to the feeding station in the bright moonlight. I munched heaps of wombat granola and thought of Chance, and hoped he was enjoying his food, too. The lights were on inside and I peeked through the sliding glass door. Donna was on the couch by the wood stove, and she was feeding a pinky. I watched quietly for a while. Then, as I walked home, I made four wishes on the wishing star (I don't think there's a rule about how many you can make, and anyway I don't really care—no more human rules for me!):

1 **For that little pinky:** May he or she grow healthy and strong, like I did.

2 **For my mum:** May she know, some way, somehow, how lucky I got.

3 **For Donna:** May she be able to sense our thank-yous from way out here. Also, may she and Phil get a few good nights' sleep once in a while.

4 **For Chance:** May he enjoy bush life safely for many more years. May he stay far away from roads. May nature be as kind to him as it was to me. May his habitat remain wild and generous and gentle . . . just like him.

I don't need human hugs anymore!

I'd always wished to meet a real wombat. Unfortunately, they only live in one place—all the way across the planet in Australia (I live in New York City). But my wish finally came true when I boarded a plane for a twenty-hour flight to the land down under. And a few days later, I got to touch my first wombat, a gorgeous golden female named Dawn. Everything moved in slow motion. The experience was pure starshine.

Wombats have been my favorite animal since I was a teenager. Somehow I feel connected in a big, mysterious way to these charming marsupials. So I was thrilled to spend many days and nights observing and interacting with the creatures of Sleepy Burrows—"where wombats dominate and humans accommodate."

Thanks to the hospitality and generosity of Donna, Phil, and their two lovely daughters, Jade and Becca, I got to walk wombats every day, shimmy my whole body into a wombat's cool, damp burrow, give a wombat a warm bubble bath, and stay up all night long with Lucy, a playful baby wombat.

As I drove away from my visit to Sleepy Burrows, it was dusk. Three stars shone in the big Australian sky. And so I made three wishes:

- I wished to help the wombats in any way I could.

- I wished to write a book that would inspire readers to recognize that even the oddest creatures deserve our compassion and protection. I decided I would protect them with my paragraphs, build them sanctuaries out of sentences.

- And I wished that every reader of this book would get the chance to meet the animal of their own dreams!

— Kama Aishrun

THREE QUICK QUESTIONS FOR DONNA STEPAN

Q: What do you say to people who think your life with thirty wombats is pretty odd?

A. *I would say they're absolutely right. My life isn't normal. My life is far from normal. When I started the sanctuary, everyone told me I'd lost the plot. But for me it's heaven. I wouldn't have it any other way.*

Q: If wombats could talk, what would be the most important thing they could tell humans?

A: *I live here too. Please drive slowly. Please find ways to live gently beside me and the other creatures, so we can all enjoy our time on this planet.*

Q: Running a sanctuary is tough. Is it worth it?

A: *Yes. Because people can make a difference. Saving one wombat won't change the world, but for that one wombat, the world will change forever. Yes, it's all worth it—the suffering, the challenges, the expense, the heartbreak. And the bruises!*

HOW YOU CAN HELP

Want to learn even more about the wombat way—
and the rescue and rehabilitation of wombats?

Visit Sleepy Burrows Wombat Sanctuary's website:
www.sleepyburrows.com.au

You can help wombats no matter where you live:

With friends, family, and classmates, share
what you've learned about wombats and the
environmental dangers they face.

Donate to Sleepy Burrows or other sanctuaries and
rescue groups. (Sleepy Burrows spends $1,000 a
week caring for wombats!)

You may live far from wombats, but there are wildlife sanctuaries all over the world for all different animals. Find some in your area, and ask a grownup to help you find out if you can visit or volunteer. You might look for wildlife rescue groups that help opossums—the only marsupials that live in the United States. Their problems are similar to those of wombats.

If you're in Australia, you can:

- Look out for sick, injured, or stranded wombats, and if you find one, call a rescue group at one of the numbers listed here: kb.rspca.org.au/Who-should-I-contact-about-injured-wildlife_127.html

- Remind grownups to drive slowly at night.

- Ask your town council to keep roadsides plowed (so wombats don't graze too close to the road) and put pipes under roads so wombats can use them as tunnels. Write to your government representatives about protecting all wombats and tell them your concerns about loss of wildlife habitat in Australia.

- Visit, volunteer at, or donate to a wombat sanctuary near you.

- Tell a grownup if you know about any wombats being mistreated, so they can report it to the police.

GLOSSARY

Conservation: preservation, protection, or restoration

Environment: the surroundings in which people or animals live

Habitat: the natural home of an animal

Marsupial: a mammal who grows in a pouch

Marsupium: a marsupial's pouch

Predator: an animal that eats other animals

Protect: to keep from harm

Rehabilitate: to return to one's natural condition

Release: to let go

Rescue: to save or help

Sanctuary: a safe place

Welfare: the health and happiness of a person or animal

HOW TO SPEAK AUSSIE

Ace: excellent

Arvo: afternoon

Aussie: Australian

Bikkies: wheat biscuits, like Wheaties cereal

Bizzo: business (as in, "Mind your own bizzo!")

Bloke: boy

Bub: baby

The bush: outdoors, the wild, anywhere that is not the city

Chokkers: full (as in, when you've eaten too many bikkies)

Chucking a tanty: throwing a tantrum

Dag: a silly creature

Down Under: Australia

Go bush: turn wild

Good on ya: good for you

Knackered: tired

Lost the plot: gotten a little crazy, out of control

Mate: friend

Nutter: a silly, goofy, or kooky person or animal

Off with the pixies: daydreaming

Oz: Australia

Spark up: perk up, pay attention

Stroppy: sassy, bossy, uncooperative

Ute (rhymes with cute): truck

Wee: small

Whinge (rhymes with fringe): whine

BIBLIOGRAPHY

Berendes, Mary. *Wombats*. North Mankato, MN: Child's World, 1998.

Daniels, Lucy. *Wombat in the Wild*. London: Hodder Children's Books, 1996.

Dennis, Linda, Kim Rolls, Anna Fowler, and Anne-Marie Dineen. "A Guide to the Care of Bare-Nosed Wombats." Fauna First Aid and Fourth Crossing Wildlife. www.fourthcrossingwildlife.com/careofcommonWombats.htm.

French, Jackie. *How to Scratch a Wombat*. New York: Clarion, 2005.

French, Jackie. *The Secret World of Wombats*. New York: HarperCollins, 2005.

Morris, Jill. *Golden Wombats*. New York: Harcourt Brace Jovanovich, 1990.

Morris, Jill. *The Wombat Who Talked to the Stars*. Queensland, Australia: Greater Glider, 2004.

Triggs, Barbara. *Wombats*. Boston: Houghton Mifflin Harcourt, 1990.

Woodford, James. *The Secret Life of Wombats*. Melbourne, Australia: Text Publishing, 2002.

WEBSiTES

Wombat Protection Society of Australia:
www.*wombatprotection.org.au*

Wombat Awareness Organisation:
www.*wombatawareness.com*

The Wombat Foundation:
www.wombat-foundation.com.au

Wombania: www.*wombania.com*

Wombat Resources: www.*wombatresources.com*

PHOTO CREDITS

Ling, Jacky: pages 3, 7, 10, 12, 16, 22, 25, 41, 54, 60, 64, 73 (lower right), 84, 86, 87, 91, 93, 107 (right), 110 (right), 112, 115, 124, 127, 149, 151

Sleepy Burrows Wombat Sanctuary (Phil Melzer and Donna Stepan): pages 9, 11, 23, 27, 29, 30, 35, 38, 43, 44, 46, 47, 50, 53, 55, 61, 69, 72, 73 (lower left), 77, 83, 88, 92, 96, 99, 101, 102, 107 (left), 110 (left and middle), 125, 129, 131, 132, 133, 142, 145

Bright, Trudy: pages 59, 74, 78, 93

Reproduced with permission from Radiology of Australian Mammals by L. Vogelnest and G. Allan, published by CSIRO Publishing, 2015: page 57

Shutterstock: page 108

ACKNOWLEDGMENTS

Heaps of thanks to:

Jade and Becca Melzer

Monica Thomas and Cynthia Coppock, sanctuary volunteers extraordinaire

Jackie French, author of *The Secret World of Wombats* and world-class wombat whisperer, teacher, and inspirer

Dr. Joseph Nowak, who has cared for so many Sleepy Burrows wombats

Photographer Jacky Ling, who captured the wombat smile and spirit

Dianne and Warwick (Waz) Bisset, of Rocklily Wombats, who introduced me to wallaroos and more wombats

Ella Dino, who gave me a kid's perspective

Roz and Kev Holme, of Cedar Creek Wombat Rescue

Evan Quartermain, of Humane Society International, for insight about habitat conservation

Gerry Hawkins and Janine Davies, of Shoalhaven Bat Clinic, who taught me more about Australian wildlife rescue

Michael Barrish and Samantha Berger, who believed in me . . .

Jay Einhorn, who wrote the poem "My Mummy's Pouch" for little Emily long ago

. . . and Erica Zappy Wainer, who welcomed the wombats onto her desktop.

INDEX

◁▽ TRUE TALES OF RESCUE ▽▷

Available now!

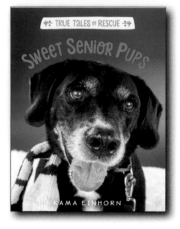

Coming soon!

Kama Einhorn is a humane educator, animal welfare advocate, and author of more than forty books for children and teachers. Animals are her people. She lives in Brooklyn, New York.